KW-176-668

Windmills: A Project Series for Young People

Strictly for the Boyds – Gail and Graeme

Windmills: A Project Series for Young People is a fresh look at one of the world's oldest machines. Windmills, the latest in the Project Series, is an entertaining way to learn how and why windmills work. From the earliest horizontal mills to the high-tech wind engines of the 20th Century, this Project Book explores both the history and the future of windpower. And because Project Books are meant for *doing* as well as *reading*, instructions for two windmill models are also included. Step-by-step instructions help the reader construct a post mill and a Savonius Rotor from ordinary, inexpensive materials.

Windmills

A Project Series for Young People

Anne and Scott MacGregor

Pepper Press, 1982

621.4
MAC

Text and Illustrations
Copyright © Anne & Scott MacGregor, 1982

All Rights Reserved. No part of this
publication may be reproduced, stored in
a retrieval system, or transmitted, in
any form or by any means electronic,
mechanical, photocopying, recording
or otherwise, without the prior
permission of the Copyright owner.

Designed by Nick Thirkell and Associates

The authors wish to thank the following
institutions for assistance: New York Public Library;
Smithsonian Institution, Washington D.C.;
Society for the Protection of Ancient Buildings (UK);
and Stavanger Maritime Museum, Norway,
Central Electricity Generating Board

Phototypeset by Tradespools Ltd, Frome, Somerset
Printed in the United Kingdom
for Pepper Press
An imprint of Evans Brothers Ltd,
Montague House, Russell Square, London WC1B 5BX

ISBN 0-237-45641-9

ilea
Library Loans Service
clrs

Contents

I A Natural Development

II Changing Direction and Appearance

III Towers and Smocks

IV Windcatchers Enter the New World

Glossary

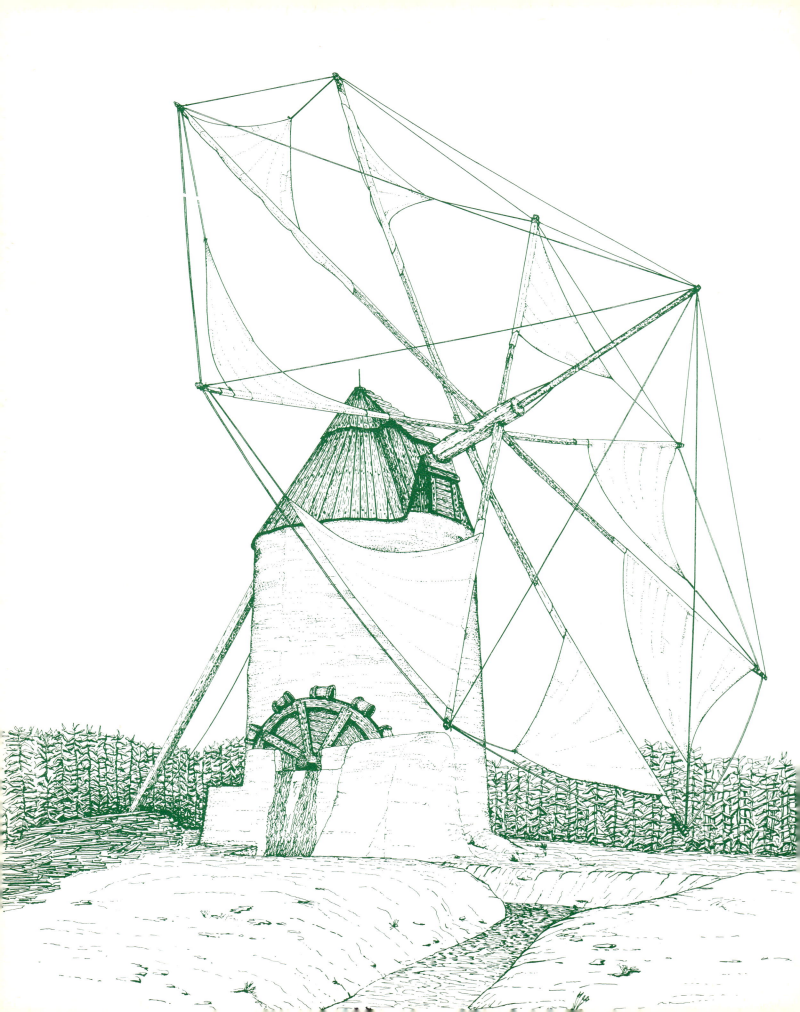

I A Natural Development

Windmills are one of the world's oldest machines. They were used to power machinery for more than a thousand years before being replaced by the steam engine. Without polluting the atmosphere or using up the world's supply of natural resources, windmills made life easier for the people who used them.

Because windmills are powered by wind, they are a good alternative to systems that use oil and other fossil fuels and minerals. Wind is free, unlimited in supply, clean and safe to use. Fossil fuels are not only expensive, they are also dangerous to use and the harmful wastes they produce are impossible to get rid of.

The development of windmills in countries as distant and different as Afghanistan and Holland is something of a puzzle, as there is no evidence that the first mills were modelled after one another. The appearance of mills varied from country to country even though they operated on the same principles.

The wind was used as an early source of energy when it was put to work driving sailing ships. The sail was introduced more than five thousand years ago in Egypt. Before its invention boats were powered with the aid of a paddle or an oar. After the sail's introduction in 2800BC or thereabouts, people could travel further and faster in bigger and safer ships. From the simple Egyptian *dhow* with its triangular *lateen* sail to the Phoenician *hippo* with its large square sails, nations used the wind to see and conquer new lands and expand their worlds.

Triangular sails on Mediterranean sailing ships were adapted for use on windmills, such as this irrigation mill in Spain. At the same time, sails on Chinese mills looked like those on *junks*. The similarity between ship sails and windmill sails shows a natural development in the use of wind as a source of energy that was destined to change the world.

The first windmills were *horizontal mills* and they looked like this one which still stands in the Seistan Province of Afghanistan. They were called horizontal mills because their sails move in a horizontal direction like the wind does. Such mills were surrounded by mud brick walls with openings that controlled the flow of wind. Their sails were made of matting and fixed to spokes radiating from a vertical post – very much like branches on a tree.

These two-storey mills were usually constructed on the highest ground to catch the strongest winds without interference from trees and other

obstructions. Wind flowed through the wall openings – openings that directed the wind against the sails and moved the machinery below them. Mills like this were used to grind grain, making it edible, but many horizontal mills were also used to bring water to dry land.

The inset shows: (1) The base of the vertical post at the mill's lower level. (2) The millstones that ground grain into meal or flour. (3) The *hopper* into which the grain was poured into the millstones and (4) the collection pan for ground meal or flour.

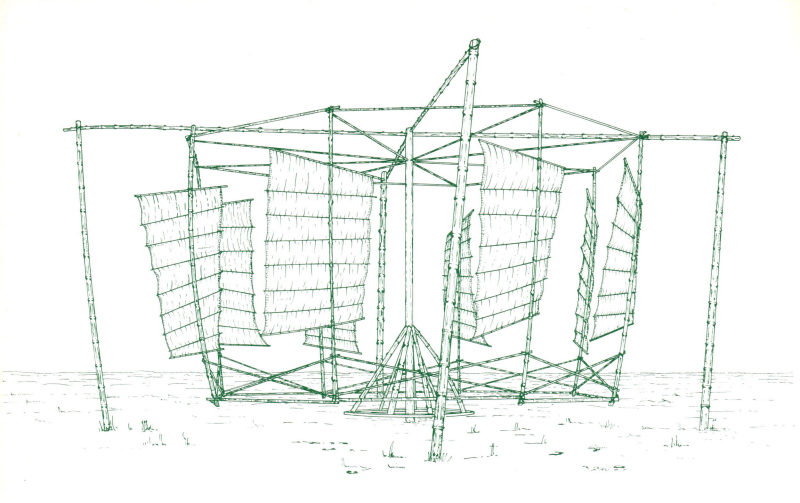

Horizontal mills were first used in China to irrigate land, particularly that which was used to grow rice, and to pump sea water into ponds where it was processed into salt.

Although these mills worked like those in Afghanistan, they looked very different. Sails on the Chinese mills were self-adjusting and were not enclosed within brick walls because they were very efficient in catching the wind throughout the year, no matter which direction it came from.

Each sail was covered in lightweight cotton fabric and attached to a bamboo arm. Sails turned on their own axis while moving like a merry-go-round around the mill's hub. By using such lightweight materials they were quicker and easier to build than their counterparts in Afghanistan. They were also portable which enabled farmers to shift them whenever and wherever they were needed.

Windmills like this one are still used in China. They power simple pumps for drainage and irrigation, making the individual and the community less dependent on more complicated technology and expensive, imported sources of energy.

Beginning and the End

Long before horizontal mills, food was made by pounding and crushing grains by hand. The earliest grinding was done with a *pestle*, a hand-sized stone that was used to pound grain into a stone container called a *mortar*.

MORTAR AND PESTLE

The next development in the manufacture of food was the introduction of the *quern*. Querns were basically two round stones between which grain was ground. The top one was rotated over the bottom one which was fixed in place. This movement broke the hard shell of the grain, grinding it and its centre kernel until it was edible. A further development, the *rotary quern*, had a wood handle attached to the top stone which made the job of turning the stone more convenient.

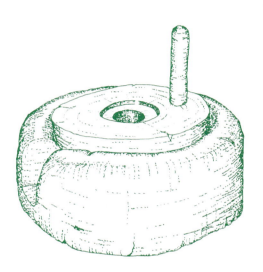

ROTARY QUERN

Though this method of making food worked, it was tiresome and time-consuming. It was soon replaced by mills which used animal, water and wind power. The first horizontal mills that were powered by these sources of energy, had their stones above their sails or paddles (watermill). After trial and error, the position was reversed and has remained that way ever since.

Horizontal mills like those in Afghanistan and China were the final development of the primitive windmill. They were the end of one story about windmills and the beginning of another.

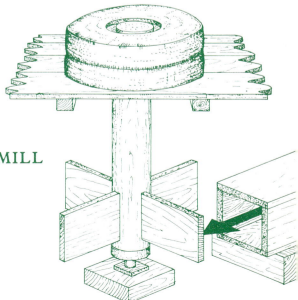

EARLY WATERMILL

II Changing Direction and Appearance

Windmills first appeared in Europe in the 12th Century. The idea of using windpower probably travelled to the Mediterranean along with the teachings of Islam, and to northern Europe by way of the trade routes from Persia.

The first European windmill was a *post mill*. They were called post mills because of the strong upright post that supported them and acted as a pivot on which the mill could be turned to face into the wind. Post mills had an average working life of two hundred years because they were designed and built so well.

Mills like this one at Chillenden in Kent, were a familiar sight in Europe and America for more than six hundred years which is a long history for any machine. Built in 1868, Chillenden Mill was one of the last post mills to be built in Britain and probably the world.

How they work

The post mill's sails were attached to the front or *poll end* of the *windshaft*. In early post mills the windshaft was nearly horizontal to the mill house, but this caused sails to sweep too close to the mill. In a strong wind sails came away from the windshaft and damaged the mill house and sometimes the miller! As a result, the windshaft was lifted so that the poll end was higher than the back end of the windshaft. This enabled sails to turn free of the mill house, while it created more space at the mill's base where the miller worked.

The sails turned in a clockwise or counter-clockwise direction to power the mill's machinery. Placed as they were, these sails were always fully exposed to the wind which made them more efficient than those on the horizontal mill which were only partly exposed to the wind at any one time. The combination of fully-exposed sails on a mill that could turn full circle to face the wind, made the post mill one of the most efficient and sophisticated machines of its time. The post mill effectively used a principle on which all windmills have since been based – at all times the sails face into the eye of the wind to make the best use of this unpredictable source of energy.

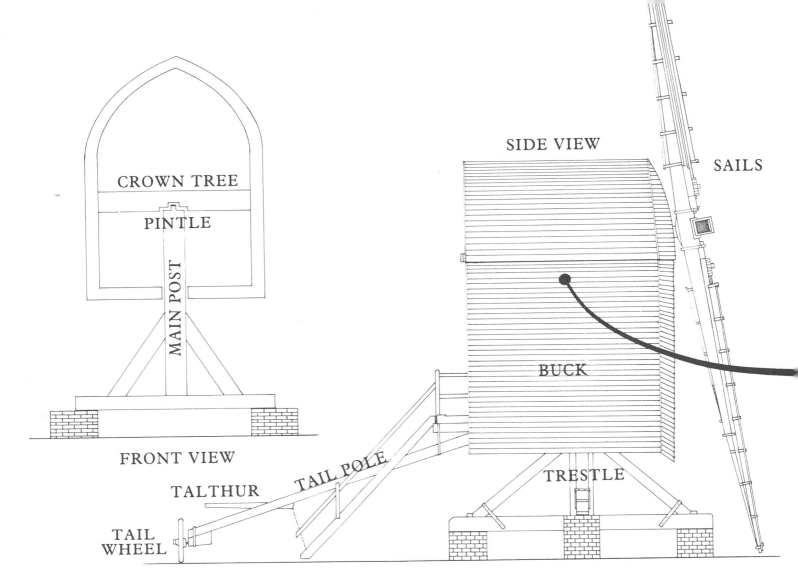

CROWN TREE

PINTLE

MAIN POST

FRONT VIEW

SIDE VIEW

SAILS

BUCK

TAIL POLE

TALTHUR

TRESTLE

TAIL WHEEL

All About the Post Mill

The most noticeable feature of any mill must be the *sails* which are also called *sweeps*. When turned by the wind, the sails drive the mill's machinery which is enclosed and protected by the *buck* or mill house. The buck's frame is covered by boards or shingles. The first post mills had pitched roofs, however, the size and shape of the mill roof changed as improvements were made to mill machinery.

The buck is supported by the *main post* which is placed slightly forward of the mill's centre because greater strength is needed to support the weight and movement of the sails. The *crown tree* is a strong beam which spans the buck's body and rests on a *pintle*. The pintle is the wedge at the top of the main post. The post mill uses this wedge as a pivot for turning the buck and the sails into the wind.

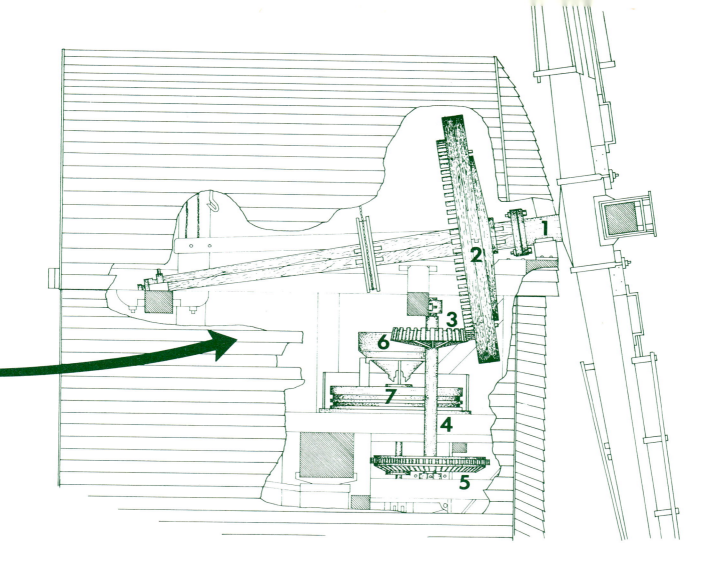

Anything below the buck is called the *trestle*. This includes the *cross trees*, *quarter bars* and *piers*. The trestle was buried below ground in the first post mills and these mills were called *sunk post mills* or *peg mills*. Mill builders later raised the post mill above ground on brick or stone *piers* to protect timbers from rotting. These mills were called *open trestle post mills*.

Animals were harnessed to the *tail pole* of the first mills to turn them into the wind. Later the *winding* was done by the miller himself because the job was made easier with a *tail wheel* on the end of the tail pole, and a *talthur*, which lifted the mill's ladder off the ground.

The sails turn the *windshaft* (1) and *brake wheel* (2). The brake wheel meshes with the *wallower* (3) which drives the *upright shaft* (4). The upright shaft turns the *great spur wheel* (5). Grain is poured into the *hopper* (6) above the millstones (7) which are turned by the great spur wheel immediately below them.

Early post mills had small bucks – just big enough to contain one set of millstones. If the workload increased, a second mill was sometimes built nearby to do the extra work. This often happened in Britain, while in Europe, existing mills were enlarged to create storage space and room for a second pair of millstones. The Briarde Post Mill at Wormhoudt in northern France is a good example of this.

These mills were simple, timber-frame buildings and wings could be easily added to them, like extensions to a house. Windows were added to provide natural light inside the mill, and a good view of weather outside. Through these windows the miller could judge weather changes and their effect on the mill's operation.

By the 18th Century, post mills everywhere had *roundhouses* around their bases. These were circular buildings made of brick, stone or timber and they protected the trestle, created storage space and provided a strong curb or base to turn the mill on. In heavier mills their walls helped support the weight and stresses on the mill's main post. Roundhouses were also used to raise the mill's sails well above the level of nearby trees and other buildings which interfered with the steady flow of wind.

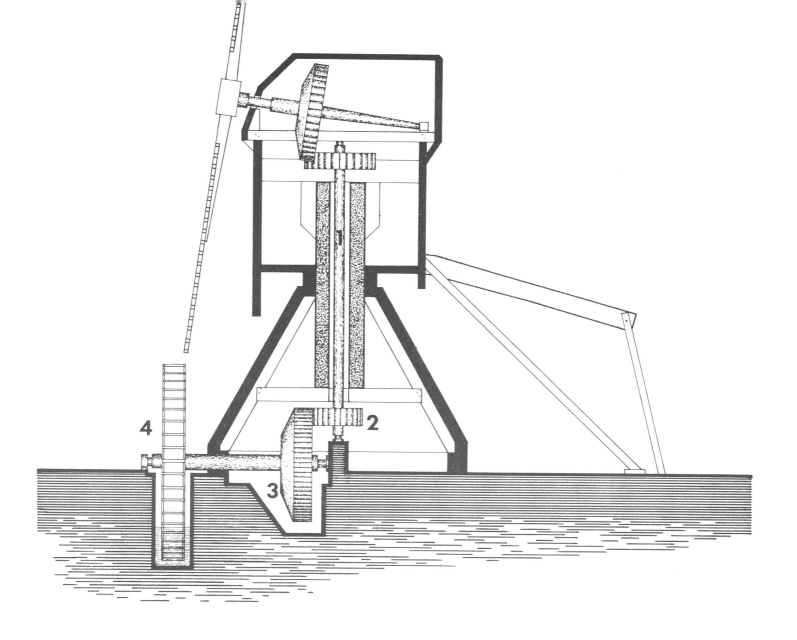

The Hollow Post Mill

In Holland, a country below sea level, the post mill was used to drain swamps and marshland to make it useful for agriculture. They were also used for grinding grains. The post mill used for drainage became known as the *wip mill* – a smaller version being the *spider mill*.

The post on these mills was hollow to allow for a *vertical shaft* (1) to pass through the mill without affecting its ability to turn full circle. At ground level the vertical shaft turned cogwheels called the *crown wheel* (2) and the *pit wheel* (3). These meshed together to turn an axle that drove a *scoop wheel* (4) which was capable of lifting seven or eight tons of water a minute at average working speed.

As the function of the post mill changed, so too did its outside appearance. The buck was made smaller because it only protected the brake wheel, windshaft and wallower. It was painted in bright colours and rested on a turning collar atop a tiled or thatched building.

Like roundhouses, these buildings covered the trestle and sometimes the scoop wheel. Since they were taller than roundhouses, they were big enough to become living quarters for the miller and his family.

Scoop wheels were first used in Dutch drainage mills to lift water and reclaim land that was otherwise useless. The technology of these mills first travelled to Britain and other parts of Europe during the 16th Century.

In later drainage mills, scoop wheels were sometimes replaced by an ancient invention called the *Archimedean Screw* which is best seen in the *tjasker*. The tjasker was a portable drainage windmill patented by Symon Hulsbos of Leiden, Holland in 1634. The sails of the tjasker (1) turned a screw (Archimedean) (2) inside a tube (3) which was submerged in a lake or swamp. As the wind turned the sails, the sails turned the screw and water was pushed through the tube and out of the lake or swamp.

Drainage mills continued to develop until the 19th Century when they were no longer needed or replaced by the steam pump. Though they became very sophisticated machines, they were developed from the simple post mill. Here are directions for making an open-trestle post mill.

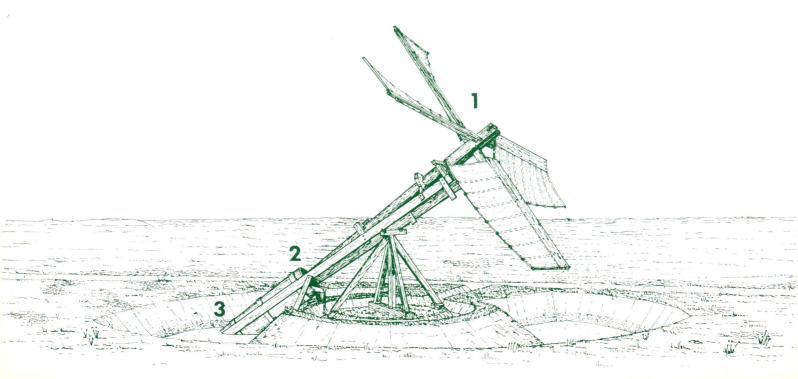

HOW TO BUILD
A POST MILL

Tools
Scissors or modelling knife
White glue
Pencil
Ruler
Paper Clips
Tracing paper

Materials
Lightweight cardboard
(2 sheets)
Medium weight
cardboard (1 sheet)
Heavy cardboard
(200 × 200mm or 8 × 8 in)
48 Wooden matches or
toothpicks
(42mm or 1⅝ in long)
2 Sharpened (new)
pencils
3 Cotton reels/spools
(32mm
or 1¼ in diameter)
4 Paper fasteners
Sticky (cellophane) tape
or masking tape

Helpful Hints
Use paper clips to hold
cardboard when gluing.
Bends are easier to make by
scoring bend lines with a
pencil. Use a ruler for
straight bends.

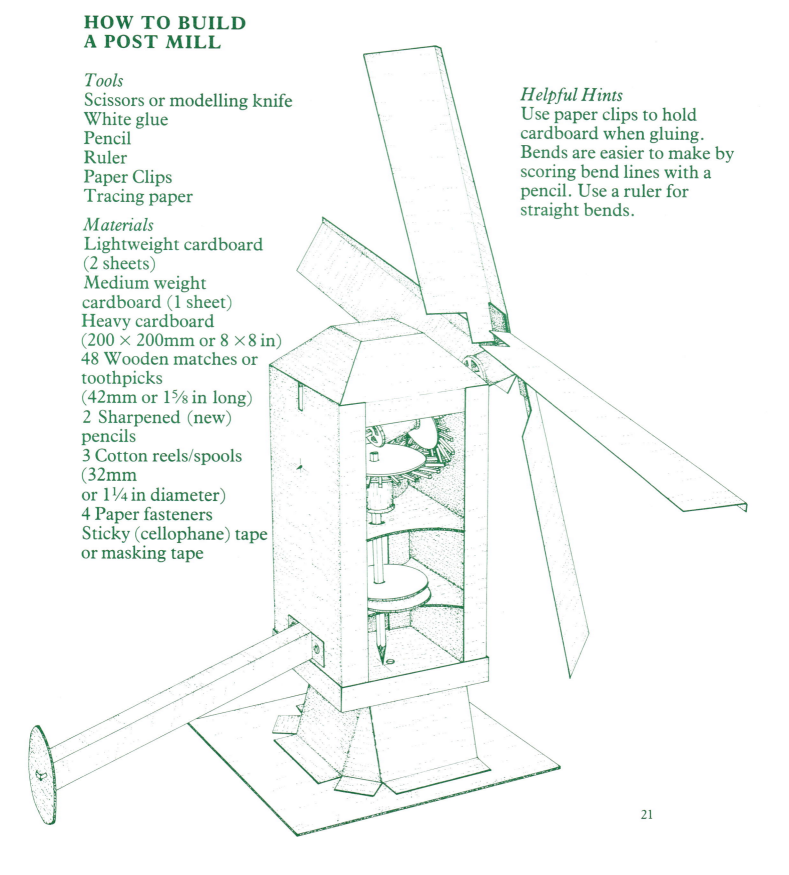

21

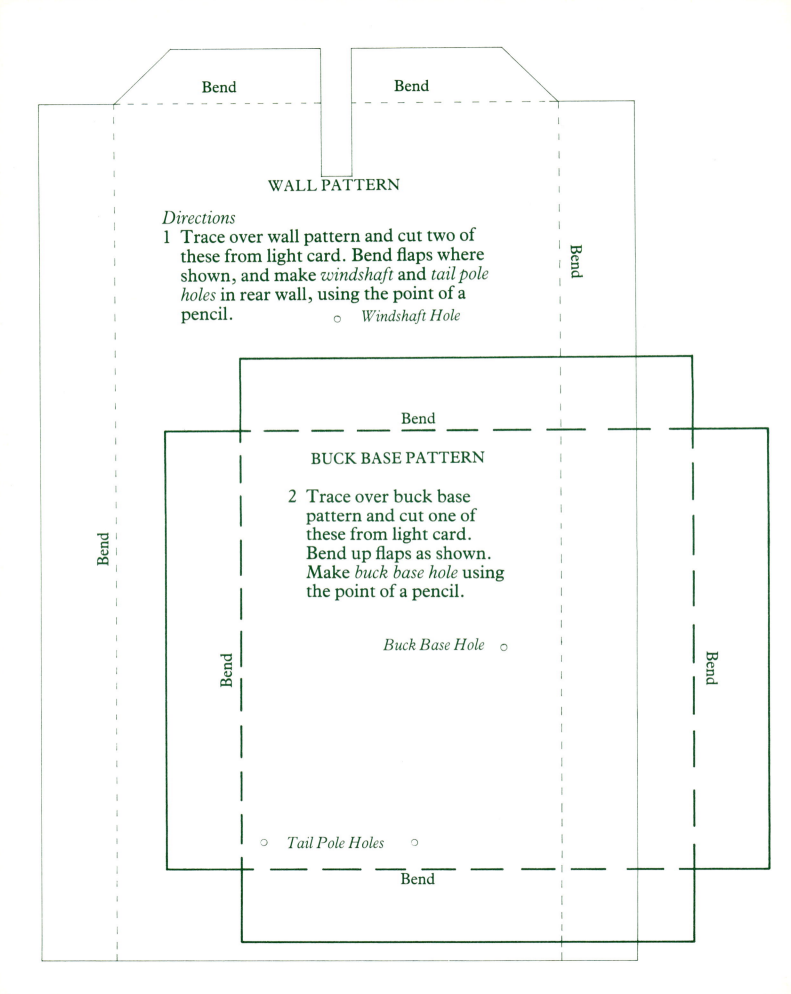

WALL PATTERN

Directions

1 Trace over wall pattern and cut two of these from light card. Bend flaps where shown, and make *windshaft* and *tail pole holes* in rear wall, using the point of a pencil.

o *Windshaft Hole*

Bend

Bend

Bend

BUCK BASE PATTERN

2 Trace over buck base pattern and cut one of these from light card. Bend up flaps as shown. Make *buck base hole* using the point of a pencil.

Buck Base Hole o

Bend

Bend

Bend

Bend

o *Tail Pole Holes* o

Bend

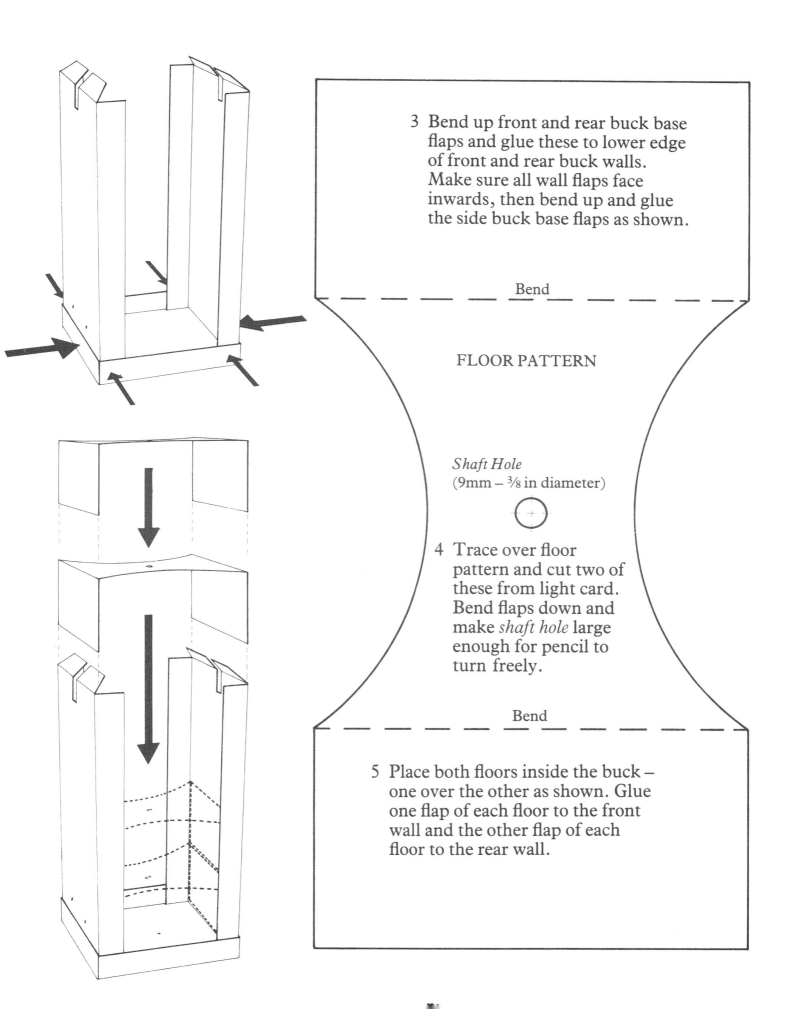

3 Bend up front and rear buck base flaps and glue these to lower edge of front and rear buck walls. Make sure all wall flaps face inwards, then bend up and glue the side buck base flaps as shown.

Bend

FLOOR PATTERN

Shaft Hole
(9mm – ³/₈ in diameter)

4 Trace over floor pattern and cut two of these from light card. Bend flaps down and make *shaft hole* large enough for pencil to turn freely.

Bend

5 Place both floors inside the buck – one over the other as shown. Glue one flap of each floor to the front wall and the other flap of each floor to the rear wall.

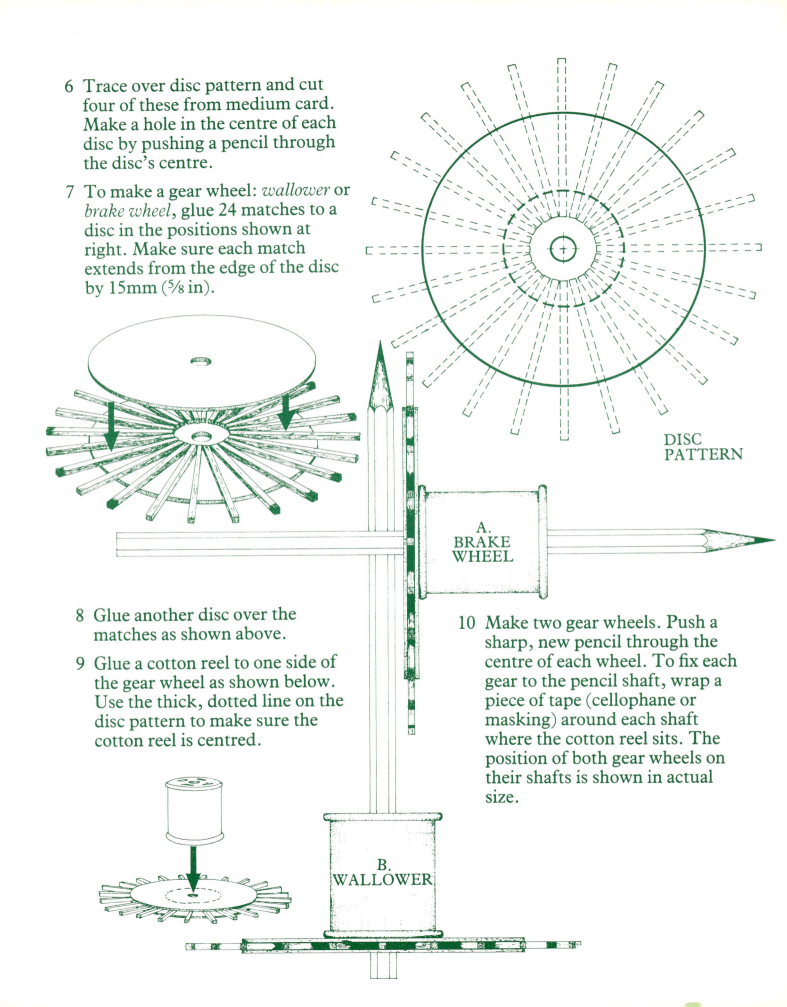

6 Trace over disc pattern and cut four of these from medium card. Make a hole in the centre of each disc by pushing a pencil through the disc's centre.

7 To make a gear wheel: *wallower* or *brake wheel*, glue 24 matches to a disc in the positions shown at right. Make sure each match extends from the edge of the disc by 15mm (⅝ in).

DISC PATTERN

A. BRAKE WHEEL

8 Glue another disc over the matches as shown above.

9 Glue a cotton reel to one side of the gear wheel as shown below. Use the thick, dotted line on the disc pattern to make sure the cotton reel is centred.

10 Make two gear wheels. Push a sharp, new pencil through the centre of each wheel. To fix each gear to the pencil shaft, wrap a piece of tape (cellophane or masking) around each shaft where the cotton reel sits. The position of both gear wheels on their shafts is shown in actual size.

B. WALLOWER

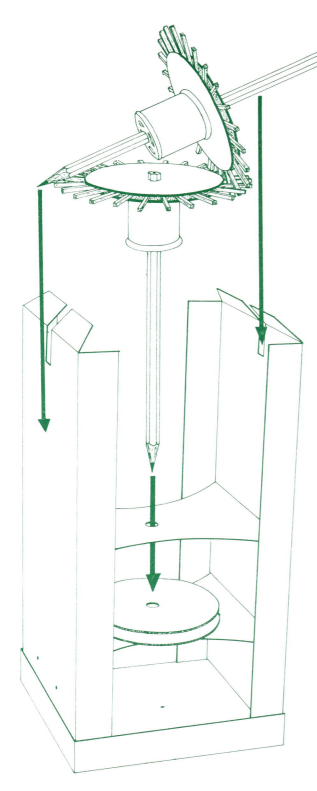

11 Use the disc pattern to cut two of these from medium card. These represent the *millstones*. Take one *millstone* and make a 9mm (⅜ in) hole in its centre so a pencil can turn easily within it. Glue this to the lower floor making sure that the shaft holes line up. This is the *bedstone*.

12 Take the other *millstone* and make a tight-fitting hole by pushing a pencil through its centre. This is the *runner stone* and should be placed over the *bedstone*. Insert (B) the *vertical shaft* that holds the *wallower*, through both floors and millstones. Make sure the *runner stone* does not slip against the *bedstone*. They should touch, but only just!

13 Place the (A) *windshaft* and *brake wheel* as shown at left so that the *brake wheel* and *wallower* mesh. You'll know these are properly placed if the *wallower* turns freely when you rotate the *brake wheel*.

14 Trace over *poll end* pattern and cut one of these from medium card.

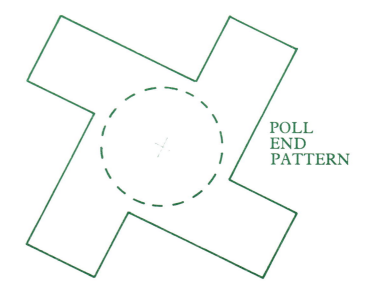

POLL
END
PATTERN

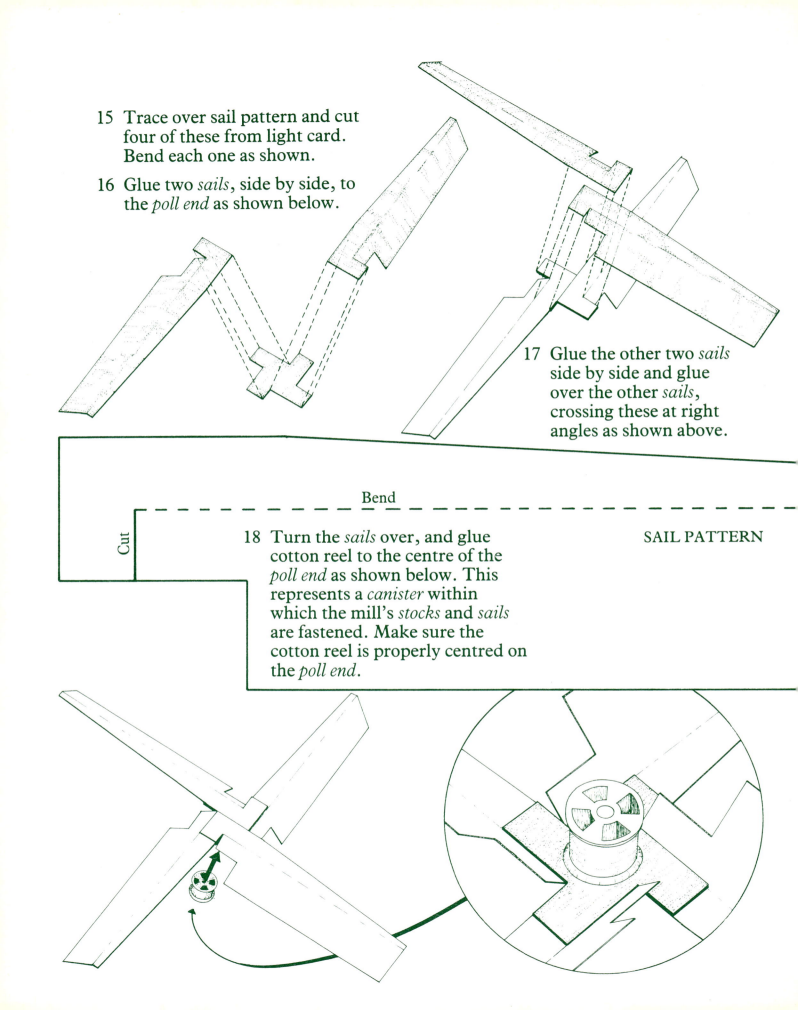

15 Trace over sail pattern and cut
    four of these from light card.
    Bend each one as shown.

16 Glue two *sails*, side by side, to
    the *poll end* as shown below.

17 Glue the other two *sails*
    side by side and glue
    over the other *sails*,
    crossing these at right
    angles as shown above.

Bend

Cut

SAIL PATTERN

18 Turn the *sails* over, and glue
    cotton reel to the centre of the
    poll end as shown below. This
    represents a *canister* within
    which the mill's *stocks* and *sails*
    are fastened. Make sure the
    cotton reel is properly centred on
    the *poll end*.

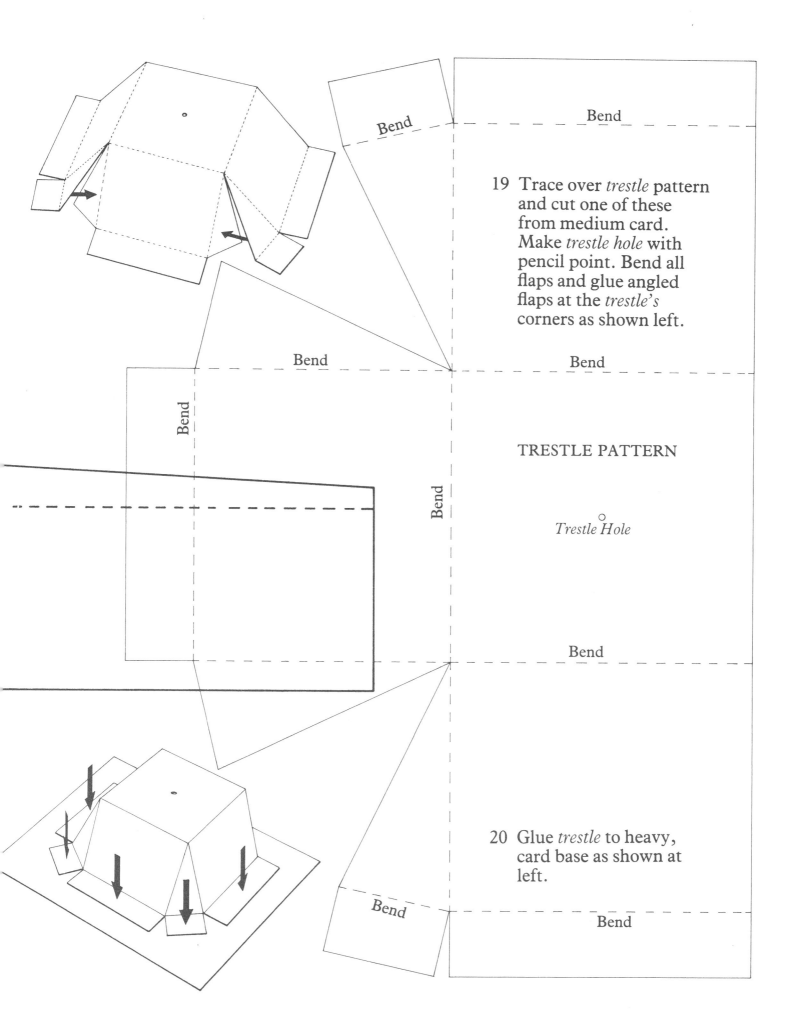

Bend

Bend

Bend

19 Trace over *trestle* pattern and cut one of these from medium card. Make *trestle hole* with pencil point. Bend all flaps and glue angled flaps at the *trestle's* corners as shown left.

Bend

Bend

Bend

TRESTLE PATTERN

Trestle Hole

Bend

Bend

Bend

20 Glue *trestle* to heavy, card base as shown at left.

Bend

Bend

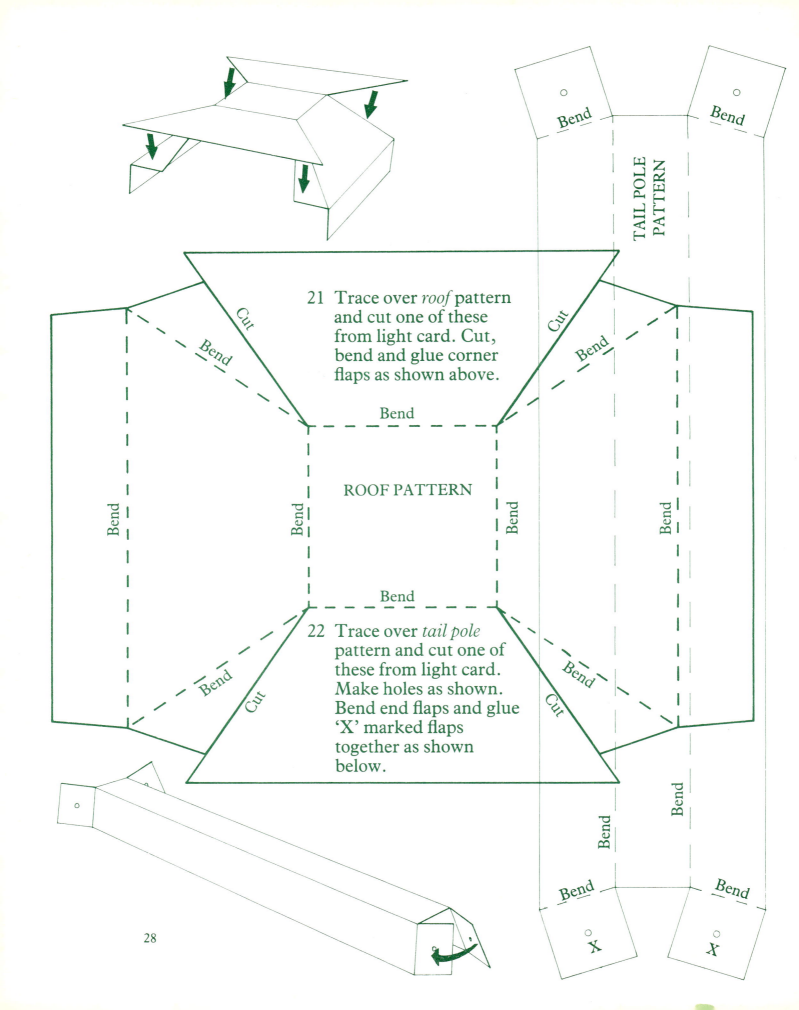

21 Trace over *roof* pattern and cut one of these from light card. Cut, bend and glue corner flaps as shown above.

Cut

Bend

Bend

Bend

Bend

Bend

Bend

Bend

Bend

ROOF PATTERN

Bend

Bend

Bend

Bend

Bend

Bend

Cut

Cut

Bend

22 Trace over *tail pole* pattern and cut one of these from light card. Make holes as shown. Bend end flaps and glue 'X' marked flaps together as shown below.

Bend

Bend

Bend

Bend

X

X

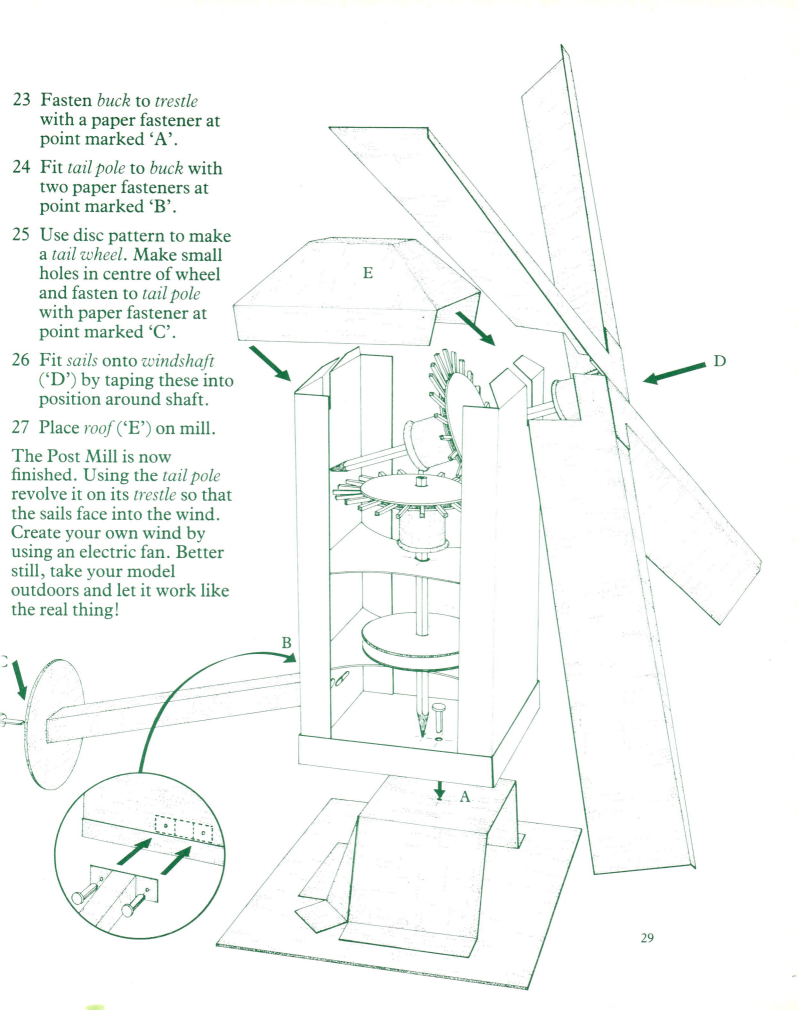

23 Fasten *buck* to *trestle* with a paper fastener at point marked 'A'.

24 Fit *tail pole* to *buck* with two paper fasteners at point marked 'B'.

25 Use disc pattern to make a *tail wheel*. Make small holes in centre of wheel and fasten to *tail pole* with paper fastener at point marked 'C'.

26 Fit *sails* onto *windshaft* ('D') by taping these into position around shaft.

27 Place *roof* ('E') on mill.

The Post Mill is now finished. Using the *tail pole* revolve it on its *trestle* so that the sails face into the wind. Create your own wind by using an electric fan. Better still, take your model outdoors and let it work like the real thing!

III Towers and Smocks

The workload of rural mills increased by late 18th and early 19th Century, while at the same time many mills were built in crowded towns and fitted with industrial equipment. As the need for milling and storage space increased roundhouses increased in height. Bucks became smaller, particularly those on drainage mills, until the traditional post mill all but disappeared. In its place came larger and more versatile wind machines called *tower mills* and *smock mills*.

Tower and smock mills rose to great heights to provide space for new machinery and storage, and to lift sails high above the roofs of nearby buildings. Apart from being bigger, the parts that moved on these mills were different from those that moved on post mills. Tower and smock mills were too big and stood too close to other buildings to be turned into the wind like the post mill. So sails, windshaft, brake wheel and wallower were fitted into a cap that could be turned full circle on top of a permanent structure made of stone, brick, timber or a combination of all three.

These caps came in all shapes and sizes depending on the country and the region. Though they supported the mill's main driving equipment, they also protected the mill from the weather, much like the roof of a house. The Fortune Tower Mill in France has a conical wood cap that has been tarred to make it weatherproof. The sails are so high off the ground that a house and other farm buildings could be built alongside the mill.

The new mills performed an amazing variety of jobs. They continued to grind grain and drain land, but they were also used to grind mustard, pepper, spices, cocoa, dye, white lead, cement clinker, chalk for whiting, flint for china and bark for tanneries. They hulled barley and rice and pressed nuts and seeds into oil and animal food. The replacement of wood machinery with that of iron made it possible for windmills to process textiles, manufacture paper and mill timber. Bigger and better than ever before, tower and smock mills became the forerunners of the 19th Century factory.

Built of brick and capped with wood, the seven-storey Berney Arms Tower Mill at Norfolk, soars 21.3m (70 ft). This late 19th Century mill was mainly used for drainage. Its scoop wheel, built alongside the tower, lifted water 1.5m (5 ft).

Berney Arms was also an *edge mill* which ground clinker (brick and rock) for the manufacture of cement. Edge mills were unlike traditional grinding mills. They ground harder, larger materials with the edge of their stones – a pair of these travelling on their sides around a stone pan. Traditional millstones were set horizontally. The top or *runner stone* crushed grain between it and a stationary *bed stone* or *ligger*.

The cap of the Berney Arms Mill turned automatically with the help of a *fantail*. The fantail is a small windmill attached to the cap, at a right angle to the sails. As the wind spins its lightweight vanes, the fantail pulls the cap along a *curb* around the top of the tower, until the sails face into the wind. The fantail stops once the sails are in motion. It moves again when the wind changes direction.

The fantail was invented in 1745 by Edmund Lee, a British engineer. It was added to late post mills and most tower and smock mills in Britain and those in Europe and America.

The fantail was not as popular in Holland as it was elsewhere. Dutch millers winded their mills by hand. *Binnenkruiers* or *inside winders*, turned by way of a *winch* or hoist from inside the mill. However caps on *buitenkruiers*, were turned by a capstan wheel attached to the mill's tail pole. The tail pole rested on a gallery or *stage* midway down the tower. From the stage the miller could set the sails and wind the mill.

The Falcon Tower Mill, built at Leiden in 1743, was called a *stellingmolen* – a mill with a stage. It was also called a *buitenkruier* because of its winding device. The miller used his own weight to turn the cap of this enormous mill. He stepped on the spokes of the *capstan wheel* and in so doing, hoisted the cap's chain which was also attached to the tail pole.

The many-sided smock mill had a timber body that rested on a brick base. The base raised it off the ground to protect timbers from rotting and to make the mill higher and therefore better able to catch the wind. Smock mills were lighter than tower mills so they were built on soft soil that couldn't support heavy tower mills. They were popular in Holland and low-lying areas of Britain and France for this reason.

In Holland, scoop wheels and Archimedean screws were built into thatched smock mills. These were known as *polder mills*. They drained and protected *polders*, low-lying land, that was otherwise subject to flooding.

Draining land with a scoop wheel was limited in depth by the small diameter of the wheel. 1.5m (5 ft) was the maximum depth. However the Archimedean screw could be made long enough to drain land up to 5.2m (17 ft) deep. For this reason polder mills with Archimedean screws worked by themselves, while those with scoop wheels were frequently used in groups or *gangs*.

These groups of mills were called *gangmolen*. They drained polders by lifting water into canals in stages. As water flowed through each mill, a *weed screen* (1) protected the mill's machinery from being damaged by floating debris. The scoop wheel (2) pushed water through a one-way gate called a *sluice* (3) while lifting it to a higher canal or the *tail race*, the downstream side of the mill.

Dutch engineers such as Simon Stevin and Jan Adriaaszoon Leeghwater pioneered this method of land reclamation in the 17th Century and through the efforts of their countrymen, Humphrey Bradley and Cornelius Vermuyden, these techniques travelled to France and the eastern counties of Britain where they were used to make hundreds of thousands of acres useful for agriculture.

Cap, sails and much of the smock mill's machinery was supported by *cant posts*. These vertical posts, at the mill's corners, spanned the distance between base and cap with one long piece of curved timber. They also gave the mill a flared shape like the peasant's smock they were named after.

The curved body and broad base of the smock mill provided a large working, living and storage space at the bottom of the mill. It also made the mill stable and strong.

Joints at the smock mill's corners were difficult to seal. As a result, smock mills were painted, sealed with tar, or thatched with reeds to protect them from the weather.

Without constant care however, they quickly deteriorated, which is why so few old smock mills remain. The 22.5m (75 ft) Union Mill at Cranbrook in England was built in 1814. Today this mill is used only for storage. Its sails are a reminder of a very busy past.

Paltrokmolen, wind-driven sawmills, first appeared in Holland in 1592. These mills were based on the design of the smock mill, but the winch and capstan wheel rotated their entire body into the wind, not just their cap. Paltrokmolen made sawn timber available throughout Holland and became responsible for the development of a style of housing that depended on wood planks and shingles. When these sawmills were adopted by North Americans in the 17th Century they carried on a tradition of timber housing which still exists throughout America and Canada today.

IV Windcatchers Enter The New World

By fortunate coincidence, the east coast of America, Canada and islands of the Caribbean, were colonised by Europe's master windmill builders. As such, these useful machines were put to work developing the new world by adventurous and enterprising people with hundreds of years of windmill experience and tradition behind them.

Stone tower mills were built by French settlers in Canada. Apart from grinding corn, these mills were also used as defensive towers. Within their thick walls, designed with openings just big enough for the barrel of a gun, these mills became a safe retreat during skirmishes with Indians and British neighbours.

Post and smock mills were constructed in America, partly because of the abundance of timber, partly because this material was favoured by both the British and the Dutch who settled the original colonies. New York's skyline, now world famous for its steel and concrete skyscrapers, was once host to rows of Dutch mills which ground grain, sawed timber and served storm warnings to seamen. In 1680 a law was passed in New Amsterdam (New York) that prohibited small craft from crossing the East River, between Brooklyn and Manhattan, when windmill sails were taken in.

Meanwhile, Danish and British settlers constructed stone tower mills to grind grain, pump water and most important – to process sugarcane in Antigua, Barbados, Curacao, Montserrat, St. Vincent and the Danish Virgin Islands. Hundreds of years earlier, Egyptians had pioneered the milling of sugarcane. It is not surprising therefore, that Egyptian experts travelled so far from home to supervise the construction and operation of these cane-crushing mills.

In America, as in any developing country, people were called upon to adapt their skills to meet the needs of the situation. Whereas most European millwrights started life as carpenters, America's millwrights learned their trade by the sea – either as ships' carpenters or captains who were skilled in shaping timber into strong and stable structures that worked *together* with nature – specifically the wind. That mills such as this one in Rhode Island have survived for almost two hundred years, is evidence of the craftsmanship that went into early American mills.

By the late 18th Century the windmill's wood gears were replaced by those made of iron. Millstones were replaced by metal rollers that were cheaper to make, easier to care for and more efficient in grinding grain to a finer texture in less time. Alterations were also made to the mill's sails. The open, wood frame of the cloth-covered *common sail* (1) was re-shaped into a sail with a curved, *leading board* (2). These sails, also covered with cloth, generated more power than earlier sails. They also moved through the air with greater ease because of their aerodynamically-sophisticated shape.

In 1772, Scottish millwright, Andrew Meikle, introduced a shuttered sail, adjusted by a spring-tension device, that used no cloth sail. In 1789, British inventor, Stephen Hooper, designed sails that used roller blinds instead of shutters. Though the miller wasn't required to climb the ladder-like frame to adjust cloth sails, in both he still had to stop the mill and interrupt his work to fix the mechanics of these shutters and blinds.

The final development of the traditional sail came in 1807 when British inventor, William Cubitt, patented a shuttered sail that was fitted with an automatic adjustment device (3). Without stopping the mill, shutters of the *patent sail* could be closed by remote control to create more sail area when there was little wind, and opened for less sail area to slow them down when there was too much.

Interestingly, these developments had little effect on mills outside Britain. Patent sails were too heavy and too complicated to be as powerful and as easy to care for as traditional cloth-covered sails. When they were used, it was in combination with common sails.

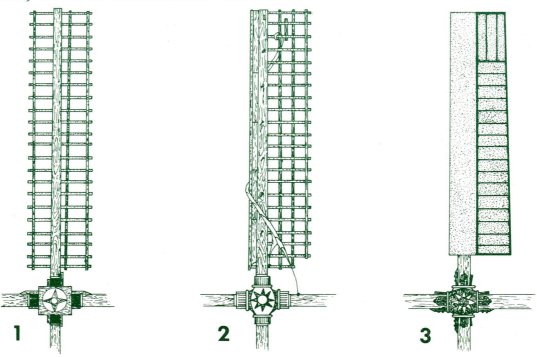

1   2   3

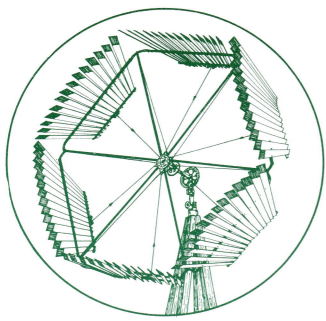

By the beginning of the 19th Century, countries on both sides of the Atlantic participated in an Industrial Revolution. This revolution brought the world prosperity as a result of changes made by new inventions. Many of these inventions were, however, powered by steam. As a result, windmills were used for fewer jobs and research into windpower was very limited for almost fifty years.

In 1850, an American mechanic, Daniel Halliday, invented a windmill that was to become the basis of the *American farm windmill* – a type of windmill still in use today.

The Halliday windmill had thin, wood blades that were grouped in sections. These blades revolved around a central hub that was attached to a vertical shaft through which power was transmitted to work water pumps and other mechanical devices. By a system of weights, the mill's sails opened and closed like a 'rosebud' presenting as much surface area as was required to efficiently power the mill. For example, in a light wind the sails were flattened, while in a strong wind they folded back.

Early American windmills were used mainly to grind corn, therefore the mill's body had to be large enough to accommodate the *food factory* inside. After 1850 however, practically all windmills built in America were designed to pump water. These new mills had no millhouse because none was required. Their towers were meant to raise sails high into the wind and support a shaft that bored into natural springs below ground. They worked by means of an up-and-down moving pump that sucked water into a storage tank when the sails of the mill were turned by the wind.

Such mills brought running water into homes in cities without water systems and homesteads in rural areas. These mills were also responsible for the development of cattle industries in North America, Australia and Argentina, where they provided water for livestock, grazing on dry, remote ranges.

The American Farm Windmill became known as the *fan mill*. Its use extended to the development of railroads, pumping water into station holding tanks for steam-powered locomotives. It also contributed to the development of vast lands these railroads opened up for agricultural development.

Only ten years after Daniel Halliday invented his mill, the American windmill industry was booming. Travelling salesmen and mail order catalogues advertised these machines and made them available throughout the country and overseas. By 1889 eighty factories were producing tens of thousands of mills that were cheap, easy to build and long lasting without much maintenance. By the turn of the century the fan mill had become one of the country's major exports. By 1930, more than six million were in operation throughout the country.

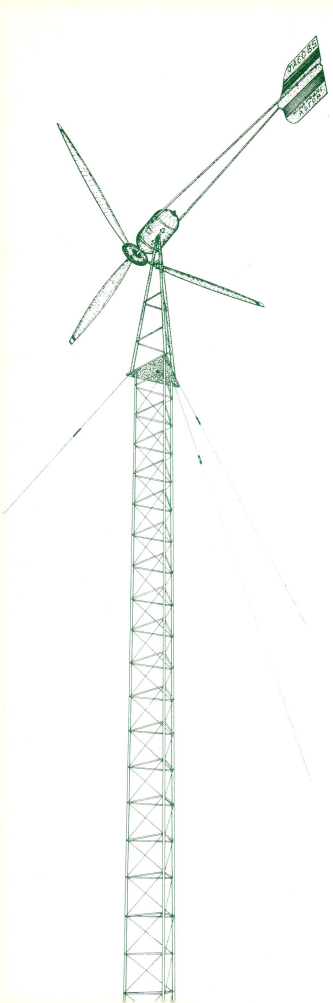

Because of its large sail area, the fan mill was considerably powerful even in light wind. These mills were so powerful they could generate enough force to pump water as soon as their fan began turning. Such mills had what's called *high torque* – great rotary force at a low number of revolutions.

However, to generate electricity, which soon became the goal of people living in rural areas, a new windmill had to be designed. A windmill with *low torque* – one with a small sail area that could spin very fast.

The earliest research into wind-powered electricity began in 1894 in Denmark by physics professor, Poul La Cour. La Cour's work was followed by that of his countryman, Christian Sörensen, who designed a mill with fewer and smaller blades than that of the fan mill.

By 1927, Joseph and Marcellus Jacobs, sons of a Montana rancher, developed a wind-powered generator that became known as an *aerogenerator* – a wind machine that was to continue its usefulness until the 50's when it became uneconomic in the face of low-cost (at that time) fossil fuels. The Jacobs' generator, designed to be efficient at very fast wind speeds, had three narrow blades that looked like an aircraft propeller. Each blade was shaped like an aircraft wing with a rounded leading edge that tapered down to a thin trailing edge. To control the speed of the blades, and thereby regulate the flow of electricity, the generator was fitted with a *fly-ball governor* that adjusted the angle of the blades according to the speed of the wind.

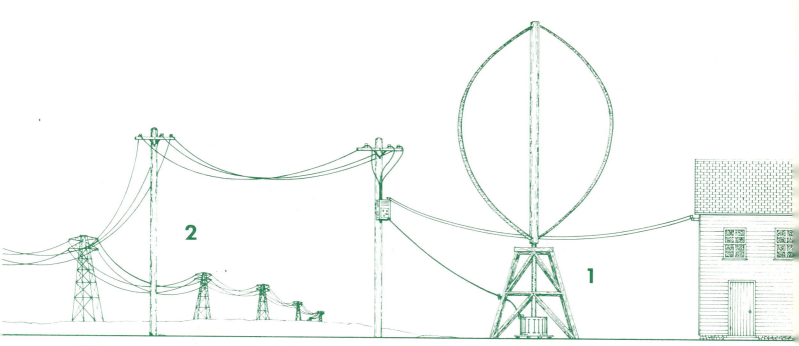

The aerogenerator solved the traditional windmill's biggest problem: how to provide a constant source of power by saving the *surplus* or extra energy generated by high winds and using it for times of little wind.

The aerogenerator and the many wind machines that followed were 'plugged in' or 'hooked up' to batteries where extra power could be stored for later use. This system, called *battery storage*, was developed after experiments proved that the energy produced by the fan mill could be stored in a car battery. The problem with this system however, was that it could only supply *direct current* (DC). While direct current could drive an automobile or illuminate a light bulb, it could not operate modern appliances like toasters and televisions. These relied on *alternating current* (AC). To convert DC to AC an *inverter* was used. These inverters however, used electricity themselves which defeated the purpose of the exercise.

Today, a highly-sophisticated system has been introduced to convert DC to AC without using extra energy. It is called the *synchronous inverter* and it works like this: The wind machine (1) fitted with a synchronous inverter is connected to a power grid – a publicly-owned power network (2). When it produces enough power for its own requirements the system is described as self sufficient. When it produces more power than it needs, the extra power is automatically put into the power grid for use by other customers. However when it is unable to produce enough power the system is *synchronized*, automatically timed, to draw the required amount of power from the grid. Such a system eliminates the problem of wasted energy, makes users self-sufficient at a lower cost, and helps the community to share those resources that are available at any one time.

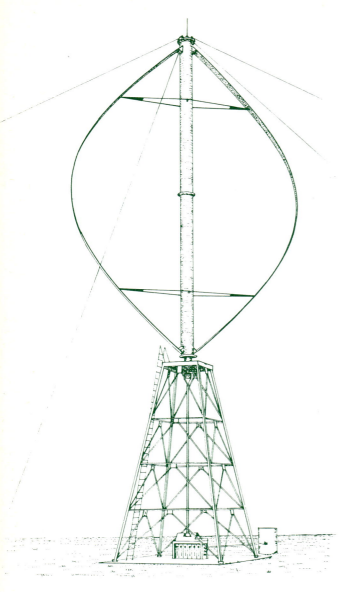

In the 1930's, the American government's subsidized Rural Electrification Administration (REA) provided cheap power to anyone who wanted it. As a result, power lines were draped across once wide-open spaces to bring electricity to the most distant and lonely corners of the country. Apart from the eyesores created by poles and wires, the cheap power they supplied discouraged many people from using wind generators.

Since the American Government no longer subsidizes energy supplies, many people, particularly in rural areas, are looking at windmills again. They cost less to operate than electric pumps and they go right on working even when storms blow down power lines! Windmills, in combinatioin with other sources of energy, are proving to be a satisfactory alternative for the future.

Fortunately, windmill engineers were never discouraged by the world's lack of interest in windpower. Research continued and led to many new and exciting windmill designs. One of these, the Darrieus Rotor, was patented by French inventor, G.J.M. Darrieus in 1931.

The Darrieus Rotor, or 'eggbeater' as it's sometimes called, is a vertical axis mill like the Afghan horizontal mill. It turns in a horizontal direction with sails attached to a vertical axis. One of its main advantages over the propeller-type mills is that it doesn't have to be turned into the wind. The other is that it doesn't require a tower as its vertical shaft is strong enough to support it.

Another exciting mill is the Savonius or S-Rotor, which was patented by Finnish inventor, Sigurd J. Savonius in 1929. The S-Rotor is also a vertical axis mill. It has been adapted to the high technology required by the developed world as well as the simple and efficient technology needed by the developing world. Here are instructions for making an S-Rotor.

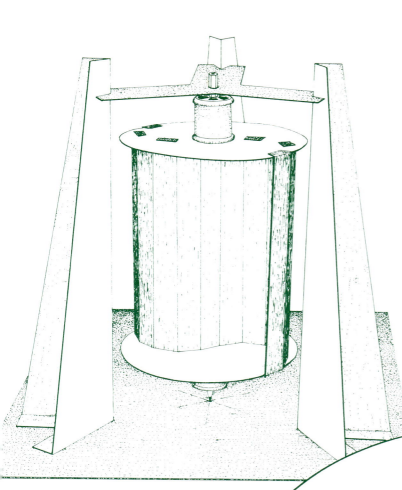

Materials
400 × 400mm (15 × 15 in) heavy-weight cardboard for base
One sheet of medium-weight cardboard at least 450 × 300mm (18 × 12 in).
One sheet of light-weight cardboard at least 600 × 450mm (24 × 18 in).
2 Cotton reels/spools, 32mm (1¼ in) diameter
2 Lengths of pencil or 7mm (¼ in) diameter dowel – both 60mm (2½ in) in length.

HOW TO BUILD AN S-ROTOR

Tools
Scissors or Modelling knife, White glue, pencil, ruler, Paper clips, tracing paper

ROTOR END PATTERN

Cut

Cut

Cut

Cut

1 Trace over *rotor end* pattern and cut two of these from medium cardboard. Cut four slots in each end, as shown.

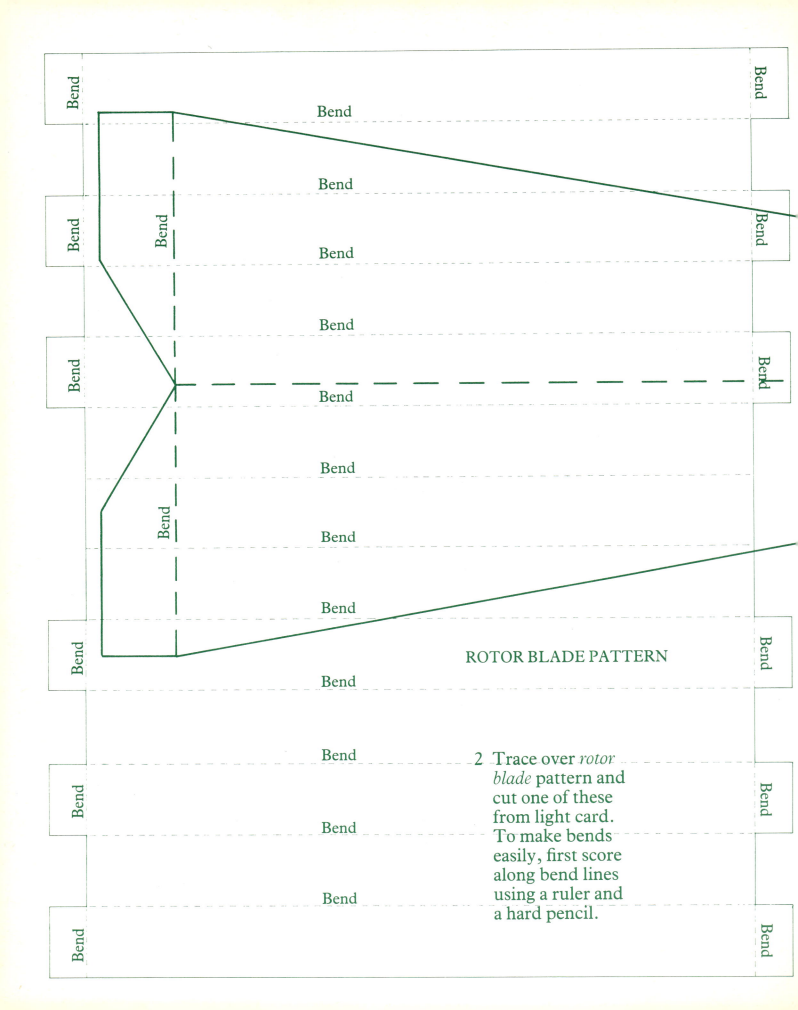

ROTOR BLADE PATTERN

Bend Bend Bend Bend Bend Bend Bend Bend Bend Bend Bend Bend Bend Bend Bend Bend Bend Bend Bend Bend Bend

2 Trace over *rotor blade* pattern and cut one of these from light card. To make bends easily, first score along bend lines using a ruler and a hard pencil.

3 Push four tabs on *rotor blade* through the four cuts in each *rotor end* as shown at right. Bend tabs and glue down *rotor ends*.

SUPPORT FRAME PATTERN

Bend

4 Bend corner tabs at each end of the *rotor blade*, folding these over the edge of each rotor end. Glue as shown below.

5 Take one pencil or piece of dowel. Sharpen one end and glue the other end into a cotton reel. Glue other pencil or dowel (unsharpened) into the other cotton reel.

6 Glue the end of each cotton reel to each *rotor end* making sure these are centred.

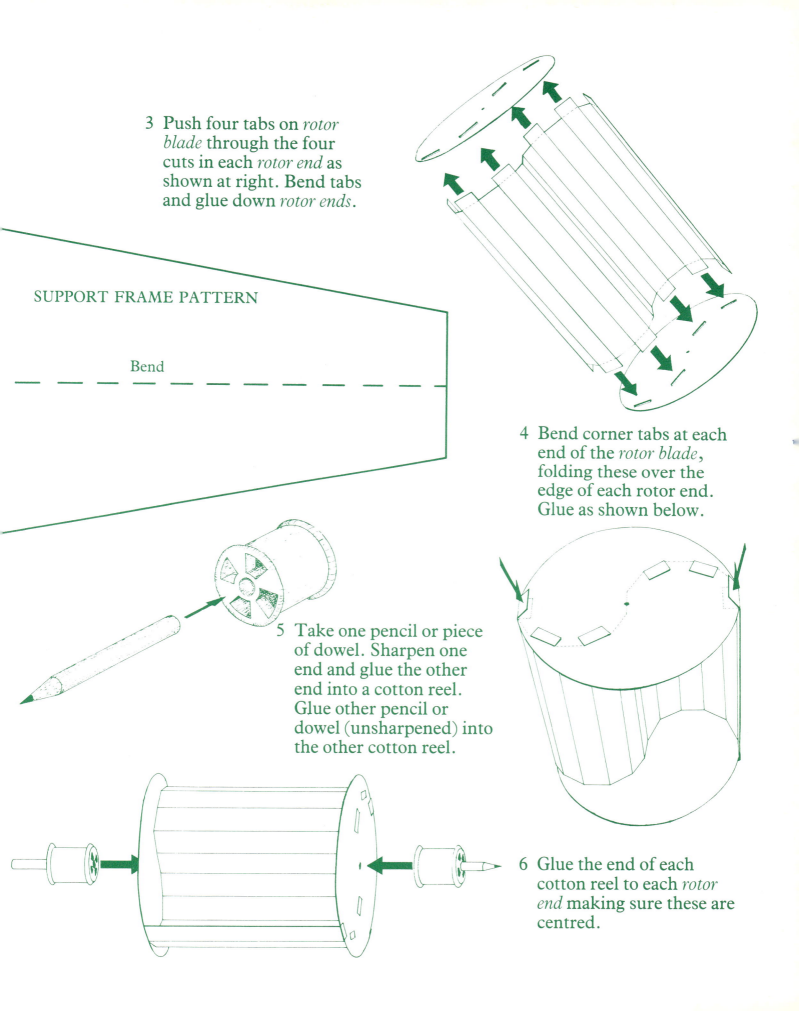

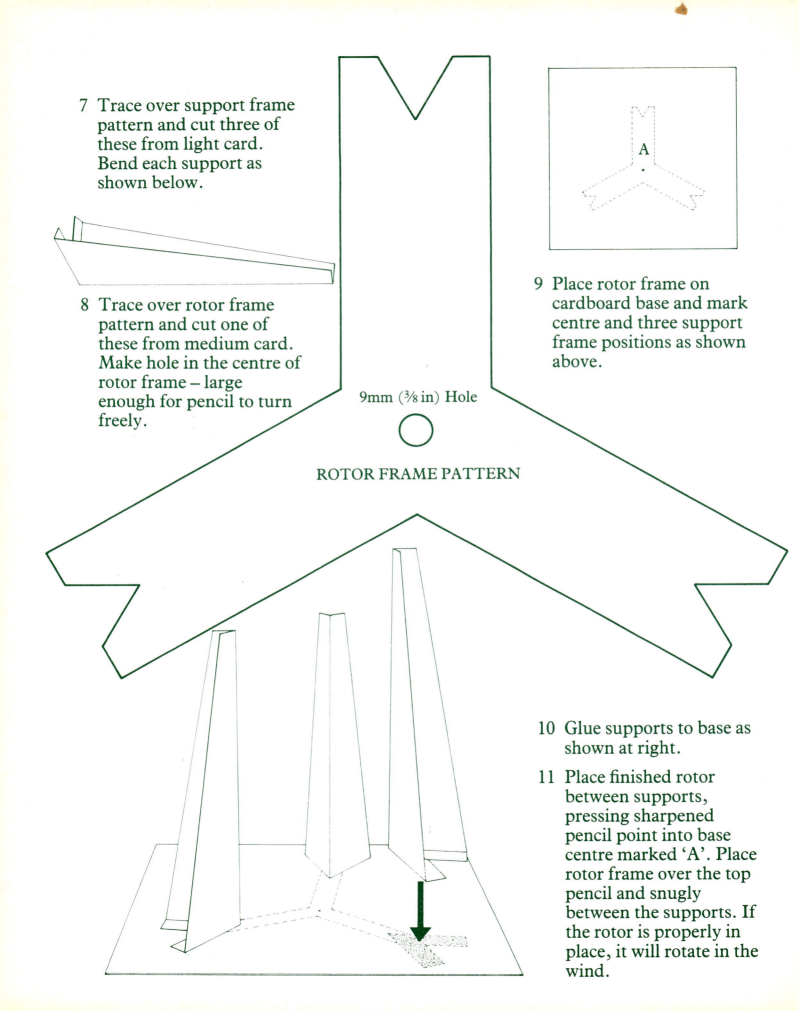

7   Trace over support frame pattern and cut three of these from light card. Bend each support as shown below.

8   Trace over rotor frame pattern and cut one of these from medium card. Make hole in the centre of rotor frame – large enough for pencil to turn freely.

A

9   Place rotor frame on cardboard base and mark centre and three support frame positions as shown above.

9mm (³⁄₈ in) Hole

ROTOR FRAME PATTERN

10 Glue supports to base as shown at right.

11 Place finished rotor between supports, pressing sharpened pencil point into base centre marked 'A'. Place rotor frame over the top pencil and snugly between the supports. If the rotor is properly in place, it will rotate in the wind.

The Savonius Rotor's S-shaped blade has a large surface area. As such these wind machines have a high torque (high rotary force at a low number of revolutions). Unlike the Darrieus Rotor, which requires an electric motor to get it started, the S-rotor will perform well as soon as its blades start turning. These wind machines were originally designed to power sailing ships. Later, they were found useful for pumping water and ventilating buildings.

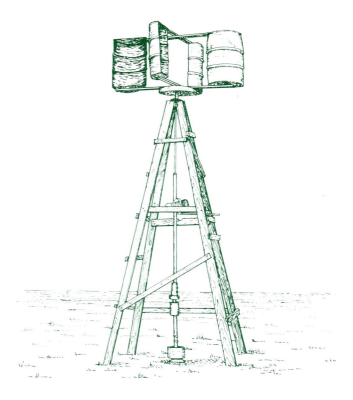

Here are two versions of the S-rotor at work. The first, made of oil drums cut in half and welded together, might be found in a developing country. In this situation the S-rotor can pump water to villages without water supplies and irrigate land for crops and livestock. Because the simple S-rotor does not require a high degree of craftsmanship to work efficiently, or sophisticated equipment that needs constant attention, these mills are ideal for use by more than half the world's population who live in the developing world today.

In contrast, the second S-rotor is combined with a Darrieus-style rotor. The highly-sophisticated result brings the best qualities of both together.

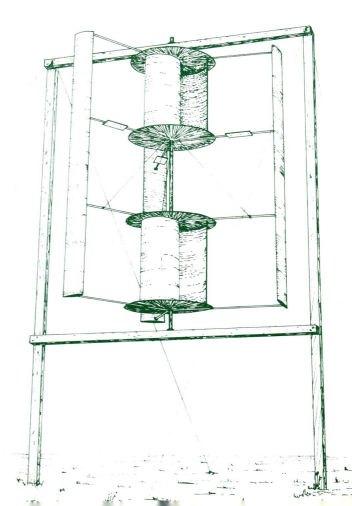

Without doubt, one of the most ambitious windmill projects of all time, was the Smith-Putnam wind turbine. This giant wind machine (left) was built during the 1940's on a 610m (2000 ft) peak, called Grand Pa's Knob in Vermont's Green Mountains.

The Smith-Putnam turbine had two enormous blades that stretched across the sky 53m (175 ft) from tip to tip. These blades, shaped like the wings of an aircraft, were raised on a 33.5m (110 ft) tower. When turned by the wind they were capable of generating 1250 kilowatts, which is enough electricity to power a small town. Early in 1945 one of these blades broke. Though the turbine never worked again, research into why the accident happened continued for many years. This on-going research led to the development of other giant wind turbines, particularly in recent years. It also encouraged the development of small wind-powered systems for a variety of jobs throughout the world.

One of these, developed by the Australian manufacturer, Dunlite Electrical, is used to power navigation lights at the entrance to Port Adelaide, Australia. One of the first windmill manufacturers in Australia, Dunlite has developed wind generators that have become a familiar sight on the continent's fertile plains as well as its arid outback.

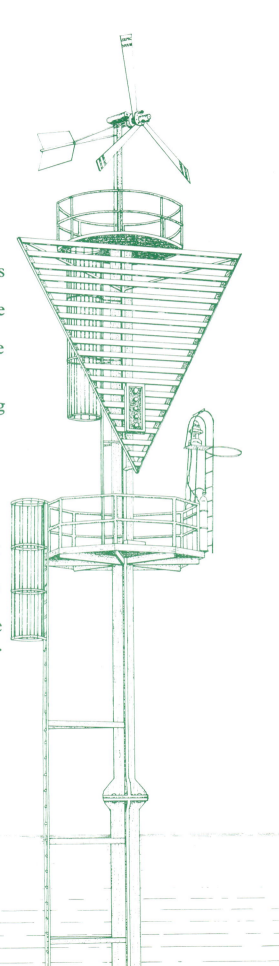

Throughout history windmills have operated with the minimum amount of materials. Their function was always more important than their appearance, so they were never burdened by architectural decoration that wasn't useful in some way. The same is true today.

This streamlined wind generator, designed for the Orkney Islands of Scotland, will produce a powerful 3 megawatts of electricity. Its sails or blades are turned into the wind by a cap that revolves around a 45m (150 ft) concrete tower when the wind changes direction by as little as 10°.

Instead of turning by way of manually-operated winches and tail poles, this cap is controlled by a microprocessor. Meanwhile, a silicon chip changes the pitch of the outer 20 per cent of the blades in the same way as the fly-ball governor changed the angle of the aerogenerator's propellers, and the shutters regulated the surface area of the patent sail.

Despite the many advances made through technology, knowledge of windpower is not that much greater than what it was hundreds of years ago. That's because the forces of nature do not change. That windmills were such sophisticated machines long before the era of high-tech, is entirely due to the resourcefulness of people who built them. As long as individuals and nations continue to use their imagination to search for better ways to use wind and other natural sources of energy, there is hope for the future.

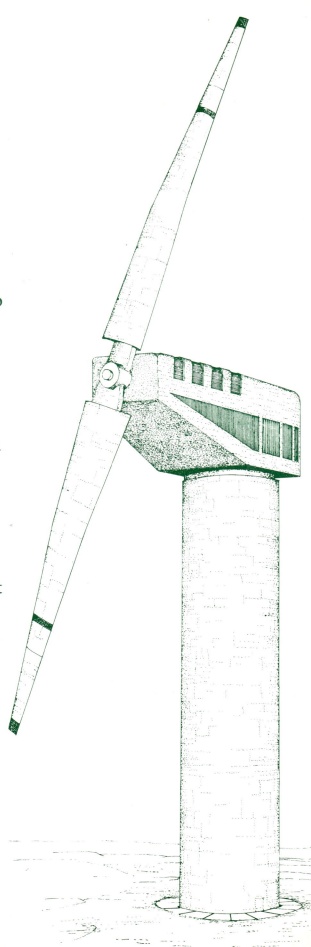

Glossary

Archimedean Screw Ancient device used to lift water. Invented by Archimedes of Syracuse (287–212BC).

Bedstone Stationary (bottom) millstone. Also called a ligger.

Binnenkruier Dutch for 'inside winder' tower or smock mill.

Brake Wheel Main gear wheel through which windshaft passes to support sails.

Buck Mill house of the post mill.

Buitenkruier Tower or smock mill in which the cap is turned by a capstan wheel on the mill's tail pole.

Canister Another name for poll end.

Cant Posts Vertical timbers on smock mill's main frame.

Cap Moveable 'roof' of the tower or smock mill.

Capstan Wheel Large diameter wheel used to turn the cap of tower or smock mill.

Common Sail Earliest wood frame sail.

Crosstrees Horizontal timbers on post mill's trestle.

Crown Tree Strong crossbeam on which the main post pivots in order to rotate the buck of the post mill.

Crown Wheel Gear wheel in drainage mill's vertical shaft.

Curb Timber rim that supports tower or smock mill's cap, and around which the cap turns.

Dhow Single-masted Arab vessel with triangular sail.

Edge Mill Mill which grinds material with the edges of its stones.

Fan Mill Another name for American farm windmill.

Fantail Small windmill used to turn mill's cap.

Fly Ball Governor A regulator fitted to the aerogenerator and other windmills to adjust the angle of the mill's blades.

Fly Tackle Another name for fantail

Fly Wheel Another name for fan tail

Gangmolen Dutch name for group of drainage smock mills.

Great Spur Wheel Wheel on vertical shaft that turns millstones.

Hippo Large sailing ship used by Phoenician merchants.

Hopper Container over millstones through which grain is poured into the stones.

Horizontal Mill Windmills with sails that turned in a horizontal direction, fixed to a vertical post.

Inside Winder Tower or smock mill in which cap is turned by a winch inside the mill.

Junk Flat-bottomed sailing ship native to China and Far East.

Lateen From 'Latin', triangular sail used in Mediterranean.

Leading Board Curved board on the edge of the sail that 'leads' into the wind.

Ligger Another name for bed stone.

Main Post Main support of the post mill.

Millstones Stones that grind material put through the mill for processing.

Paltrokmolen Dutch sawmill based on smock mill's design.

Patent Sail Shuttered sail with automatic adjustment.

Peg Mill Another name for sunk post mill.

Piers Brick or masonry foundations

under post mill's trestle.

Pintle Point at the top of the main post which wedges into the crown tree.

Pit Wheel Gear wheel that turns scoop wheel on the drainage mill.

Polder Dutch name for low-lying land that is subject to flooding.

Polder Mill Dutch drainage (smock) mill.

Poll End Cast-iron socket at the outer end of the windshaft in which the sail's stocks are held in place. Also called a canister.

Post Mill Windmill supported by a post, around which the mill's body is turned.

Quarter Bars Trestle timbers used to support main post.

Quern Hand-driven stones used in primitive times to grind grain.

Rotary quern Two circular grinding stones – the upper one rotated with a wood handle.

Roundhouse Round, low building at the base of post mills. Used for storage and to heighten the mill's sails.

Runner Stone Top millstone which revolves over the bed stone.

Sails Mill's sweeps, turned by wind to operate machinery.

Scoop Wheel Paddle wheel or wheel with scoops that picks up water in the drainage mill.

Sill Timbers on top of the smock mill's base which support the mill's frame.

Sluice One-way gate or barrier that holds back water after it's been pushed through the drainage mill.

Smock Mill Many-sided timber mill with moveable cap.

Spider Mill Small wip mill – hollow post mill. (Dutch-Spinnekopmolen)

Stage Gallery around tower and smock mills.

Stellingmolen Dutch name for tower or smock mill with a stage.

Stocks Narrow, pointed timbers attached to the poll end of the windshaft to support the sails.

Sunk Post Mill Post mill with the trestle buried below ground. Also called a peg mill.

Sweeps Another name for sails.

Tail Pole Pole attached to the back of the mill. Used for turning mill into the wind.

Tail Race The downstream side of a drainage mill.

Tail Wheel Small wheel attached to the tailpole to make moving the mill easier.

Talthur Lever on tail pole. Used to lift the ladder when post mill is rotated.

Tjasker Portable drainage mill that uses Archimedean screw.

Tower Mill Tall stone or brick mill with moveable cap.

Trestle Anything below the buck of the post mill.

Upright Shaft Vertical shaft that turns great spur wheel.

Vertical Shaft Main shaft of hollow post mill.

Wallower Gear wheel that meshes with brake wheel to turn vertical shaft.

Weed Screen Filter used to protect a mill's drainage machinery.

Winch Cable drum used to pull the mill's cap into the wind.

Winding Turning the mill's sails into the wind.

Windshaft Horizontal pole that supports sails.

Wip Mill A post mill used for drainage.